The Future of the Future

A Conscious Guide to Personal and Planetary Shift

By Laurence De Rusha

Institute for Higher Spiritual Learning,

Boulder, CO

Copyright © 2011 by Laurence De Rusha

All rights reserved, including the right to reproduce this work in any form whatsoever, without permission in writing from the publisher, except for brief passages in connection with a review.

ISBN: 978-1466385153

Second Edition, Copyright © 2013

Institute for Higher Spiritual Learning,

Boulder, CO 63017

www.larryderusha.com
www.planetaryshift.org

Copy editing and text design: Angela Renkoski

Library of Congress cataloging-in-publication data available on request isbn : 978-1466385153

Contents

Foreword 4

Apprehension 6

New Interconnected Worldview 8

Life Is About Connections 12

The Evidence of Our Disconnection 14

How We Became Disconnected 28

How to Reconnect 34

Background for Shifting Consciousness 42

The Future of the Future (background) 49

The Future of the Future Process 53

Seeding Planetary Shift 55

The Challenge 63

Suggested Reading 69

Biblography 73

The Author 80

Foreword

Imagine that you have come to the Earth from the far reaches of the universe, out beyond the beyond. Because of the travel you have forgotten your reasons for coming to this planet and you have become human, assumed the physical appearance of Earth's creature and adapted to its ways of life.

Eventually, you suffer. Events and upheavals cause pain and suffering. You long for something that calls you from the other side of the stars. You ask questions about this reality, where it began and the source. The mysteries of life seem so beautiful yet strange. Suddenly, after years of searching, you remember your previous existence and you are awakened to your cosmic self and your oneness with the universe.

(paraphrased from Sufi master, Inayat Khan)

The purpose of this book is to summarize where our current disconnected worldview has impacted the survival of the earth and its inhabitants, and to provide a simple reconnection process.

The technique presented in this book is based on Rev. Dr. Ernest Holmes' spiritual mind treatment process, and is a neuroscience based creation method, bringing together current science, metaphysics, and ancient knowledge.

Apprehension

It is a remarkable paradox that, at the pinnacle of human material and technical achievement, we find ourselves anxiety-ridden, prone to depression, worried about how others see us, unsure of our friendships, driven to consume and with little or no community life. Lacking the relaxed social contact and emotional satisfaction we all need, we seek comfort in overeating, obsessive shopping and spending, or become prey to excessive alcohol, psychoactive medicines and illegal drugs.
(Wilkinson, Richard; Pickett, Kate 2010).

Apprehension about our future is also widespread these days. Bob Dylan's lyric, "The times they are a-changin'," fits this remarkable period we are living into. Everywhere in the national media we see economic, political, and ecological firestorms. Fueled by unlimited consumption, consumerism, competition, colonization, and tribalism, these wildfires are burning out of control. Yet these are the outer symptoms of something much deeper. Beneath all of this unrest, instability, and suffering is the deep disconnection of humanity from its spiritual essence.

Other books explore in depth all the ingredients contributing to our global crisis and still others give theories on how the crises developed. (You can find some of these in the Suggested Reading section in the appendix.)

Although this book describes, in brief, the crisis-driven revolution of an old worldview (perspective), learning to reconnect and participate in a positive personal and global shift is the purpose. Our new outer world will be built on our inner awakening and a realization of our universal inter-connectedness.

Because you are still reading this, you most likely relate to what I have said and feel something profound is happening on our planet and wish to do something about it. And, like me, you might question, "What can I do? I am only one person." Well, the most significant answer to this question comes from Mahatma Gandhi when he said, "Be the change you want to see in the world."

To fully participate in facilitating such a powerful and positive change as is needed, you must go beyond the common obstacle of superficial optimism or pessimism.

Making a shift in your worldview, healing any disconnections, and positively seeding consciousness ultimately lead to shifts in the way you act, and this impacts the outer world. In other words, as you begin to shift yourself, the old materialist worldview will give way to a new worldview. Multiplied by millions, your part equals world shift!

New Interconnected Worldview

The worldview I am suggesting is actually a return to the worldview of many early indigenous and spiritual cultures, but supported by modern science. For example, author and Oglala Sioux spiritual teacher Ed McGaa stated, "Interdependence is at the center of all things. The separation between us and nature is a mirage. The perception is the result of ignorance." Similarly, in the book *Awakening,* Sufi master Pir Vilayat Inayat Khan describes the "Oneness of all."

Even the 3,000-year-old Hindu religion says we are mirrorlike jewels reflecting not separate, and not one but interconnected, like cells in the body. These old views are supported by quantum science.

"All the known fundamental particles—including the messenger particles—have properties resulting from these types of vibrational patterns. This fact is one of the most attractive and unifying aspects of string theory—it postulates that all particles are made of the same "fabric," as opposed to the particle-physics view that each elementary particle is in effect "cut from a different fabric." (Brian Greene, The Elegant Universe).

Because of this scientific detection of a "fabric" of the universe, perhaps the so-called "dark matter" or "dark energy," the more spiritual concept of interconnectedness and interdependence is more palatable to the modern Western mind.

That being said, we currently live between two worldviews. The old externally focused, ego-based worldview that attempts to manipulate material stuff to affect change, and the interconnected worldview that is inner focused on our oneness in consciousness. As Sri Nisargaddat Maharaj, a Hindu mystic, said, "There is the material world and the spiritual. Between lies the universal mind and universal heart. It is wise love that makes the two one."

Some of the dominant themes of this new perspective include:

Universal Mind: the collective unconscious in contrast to personal unconscious. Carl Jung's concept of the collective unconscious defines it as universal and impersonal in nature and identical in all individuals. This collective unconscious does not develop individually but is pre-existing in all and existent in all things. It is a compendium of all knowledge, but is nonlocal, encoded in a nonphysical plane of existence.

Intuition balanced with rational thinking: Trusting one's deeper intuitions as good guides for making decisions (along with reason).

Natural versus normal: Normal is the accepted values and behaviors in a group. It is an outside-in learning. Natural comes from a "nature" perspective, which means it is an inside-out learning. The latter knows without thinking about it that we are dependent on the earth. As many Native Americans have said, living in a cooperative, sustainable relationship with nature is critical. We must stop exploiting it for material gain.

Universal Heart: the basis of our mutual feelings of interconnection, compassion, and empathy. Although everything appears separate, the underlying phenomenon, as mentioned above, is a profound network of connections on physical, quantum, metaphysical, and spiritual levels.

Compassion: an awareness of the suffering of other human beings subjected to poverty, disease, and inhumane living conditions, regardless of who they are or where they live, and expressed as a desire to help.

Empathy: akin to compassion in its awareness of connection with others. Khen Lampert (2005) defined it: "[Empathy] is what happens to us when we leave our own bodies ... and find ourselves either momentarily or for a longer period of time in the mind of the other. We observe reality through her eyes, feel her emotions, share in her pain."

Simplicity: having the intention to leave a lighter footprint on the earth and a respect for being present. Living mindfully, or "in the Now," is given value equal to left-brained analysis and the demand to predict and control the future.

Unconditional Acceptance: the highest values of unconditional love and forgiveness in our relations with others. If we are all one, then to harm another person is to harm ourselves. The operative question in all situations of interpersonal conflict reduces to "What is the most loving thing to do?"

Life Is About Connections

Life is about connections—the connection between your conscious life, your inner Self, other people, the planet, and all else. When you are connected, you have a sense of well being, and you feel as if everything is OK now and is going to be OK.

The 3,000-year-old Buddha-avatamsaka Sutra teaches that everything is interconnected and interdependent. Lama Surya Das in his book *Awakening the Buddhist Heart* says,

Reading it [the Sutra], we think of the world as the jeweled lattice of the Hindu God Indra's web, in which each sparkling, mirrorlike jewel reflects and thus contains all the others. Like these reflecting jewels we are not separate, and we are not one; rather we are interrelated and interconnected. (Broadway Books, 2000)

This ancient view agrees with the "quantum entanglement" theory summarized by Dean Radin in his book *Entangled Minds*.

"When the fabric of reality is examined very closely, nothing resembling clockworks can be found. Instead, reality is woven from strange, "holistic" threads that aren't located precisely in space or time. Tug on a dangling loose end from this fabric of reality, and the whole cloth twitches, instantly, throughout all space and time." (Paraview Pocket Books, 2006)

Our ego mind has difficulty with concepts other than those related to the physical world. So it spends most of its time in a material, reductionist process that focuses on the parts of the whole losing site of the whole.

Surely you lose the greater perspective this way. A turbine fan blade doesn't tell much about the plane engine that it fits in and less about the plane itself. And it tells you absolutely nothing about air traffic, passengers, air controllers, etc. This viewpoint sees fragments only and fails to perceive the whole picture. So it is with life itself. Being solely identified with any one part inevitability leads to a sense of deep separation: me and you, mind and body, nation and other nations, ad infinitum.

As Jung pointed out, the resolution of this dichotomy does not take place in the rational mind. It happens on the higher levels of consciousness beyond the ego mind. It is here you rediscover your true Self? And recognize the spiritual essence of the oneness and wholeness. The higher levels are where we experience the interconnectedness or oneness.

The Evidence of Our Disconnection

To experience oneness is the Holy Grail—the quest of many sacred traditions. Yet the experience of oneness defies words and symbols. It denies description precisely because it is not an intellectual concept but an awareness and experience. For that reason, this can lead to chasing after ever-narrowing false paths.

One false path is the 400-year-old reductionist/materialist worldview. This path is fraught with a limited perspective and sees a person as a part. If you travel further on this path, you will begin feeling separate and lonely. Precisely because you don't know there is more, the whole. A few steps more and you will suffer abandonment and lose. At this juncture you also lose compassion and empathy for yourself and others, and, at its extreme, you treat everything and everyone as objects.

Sadly, most of our modern societal systems, such as the financial and political systems, are based on this type of disconnected worldview. Quite likely, this viewpoint was spun by brain structures linked to our inherited ancestral reptilian brain whose primary function is survival.

The triune brain model hypothesized by Paul Maclean, a neuroscientist, says the brain evolved over millions of years, creating three layers. The earliest is the reptilian layer, overlaid by the limbic system;

layered over and encircling the other two is the neocortex.

The characteristics of the reptilian layer are related to survival or the fight-or-flight process. But more obscure offshoots of this are competition, greed, anger, tribalism, suspicion, and violence. In contrast the modern layer, the neocortex, has characteristics that are more advanced: connection, collaboration, equality, trust.

Our world is dangerously polarized by these opposing characteristics. The evidence is clear:

- a complete imbalance of wealth and power

- crumbling economic systems

- starkly divided political systems

- a complete disregard of ecological damage.

Let's take a brief look at each of these points.

Wealth imbalance: The greed of the powerful was on blatant display for the world to see in the Wall Street crash of 2008-'09. It brought to the forefront the gap of 1 billion people consuming more than 70 percent of the material goods, wealth, food, land, and water while 5 billion people live on the rest. One recent study from the Pew Charitable Trust shows that Americans in the top 1 percent of the population now command nearly 20 percent of the nation's income. That's more than twice the share that group received three decades ago.

The deepening split between the wealthy and others is also evident in crimes against wealthy organizations. Cyber terrorism on financial institutions, according to author and cybercrime expert Misha Glenny, has been estimated to cost the global economy $1 trillion a year – almost 1.75 percent of global GDP. The hacking of Target and Neiman Marcus in 2012 compromised personal information of over 100 million customers.

The wealth imbalance surfaced most prominently in 2008 when our economic systems suffered a meltdown, and the salary and bonuses of Wall Street executives and hedge fund operators came to the forefront.

Economic-financial crisis: Greece, Italy, France, Spain, Japan, Iceland, and others have suffered from predatory financial colonialism and uncontrolled consumerism putting the Euro in jeopardy of dissolving. Only through disparate measures has it survived till now (2013).

While trillions of dollars are spent on wars, governments are borrowing from an already beleaguered populace and haggling over who's to blame.

Financial markets rollercoaster along as a result of these global issues while the so-called "free market" systems, like the stock markets, have become too complicated to manage. As a result, large computer system are now used for leverage. Programs (programmed trading) with nano-second timing and large purchases or sale blocks intentionally or unintentionally manipulate these free markets. For example, United Airlines lost $1 billion in market capitalization in 12 minutes due to this type of split-second program trading. (*The New York Times,* Sept. 14, 2008, Tim Arango).

In addition to financial markets, capitalism has mutated over time. One author calls it "gotcha capitalism." This change is about making the highest amount of money through hidden charges to consumers. The Ponemon Institute conducted a national survey in 2006 to see how much money is spent on hidden fees of various kinds (they targeted 10 areas such as cell phones, groceries, travel). The fees tallied more than $45 billion.

This complete disregard for the common sense good is another illustration of our disconnection and points to our reptilian brain's Darwinian tribalism that feeds on competition, colonization, and consumerism, which are inherently unstable.

From "gotcha capitalism" we can look at "gotcha marketing." Consumer food products and services since the 1940s have been out of control, bent on creating unnecessary demand by using advertising (TV, radio, blogs, websites, newspapers, magazines, etc.) to manipulate the consumer, through the unconscious mind, into buying a brand of products or services regardless of actual need. The result is, if the rest of the world consumed food at the same rate as the United States, we would require nine planet earths to supply the gluttony and waste.

Ultimately, attempts to stretch these old competitive and manipulative systems globally will be futile because current economic systems are so complex and unmanageable, they are easily hijacked (for example, credit default swaps), which can eventually lead to faltering economies worldwide.

As this happens, the reptilian brain reaction will cause catastrophic fear and further deterioration of the financial markets in the United States, Europe, and Asia. Due in part to greater economic confusion, we'll see further entrenchment of power circles, such as the big banks/Wall Street, and the economic manipulations of governments through lobbies in response to the need for the status quo by bureaucratic systems.

Worldwide corporate greed has become so blatant within "civilized" countries that it makes the Dark Ages look bright. These are outgrowths of tribalism, masculine competition and disconnection at its worst.

"Loyalty, of course, extended only to your tribal unit: outsiders were regarded as worthless and expendable, and if you had to kill them to protect your fellow tribesmen, you wasted no time on regret," wrote Karen Armstrong. Today, companies are concerned only about their tribe, the stockholders.

Companies no longer have visions of common good. They show little responsibility, except toward their major shareholders and highly paid officers (the 2 percent of the population). The only vision companies have is an economic one resulting in playing all angles and believing its fair; "outsiders (are) regarded as worthless and expendable."

For example, the government agencies responsible for policing and managing such ego-based corporations as Tyco, Enron, Worldcom, Chase Bank, etc., are controlled by a staff loyal to their original company and industry, their tribe. Unquestionably, this results from a lack of connection, compassion, and empathy on the part of the individuals running the companies, regulatory agencies and government.

When the main thrust of the economy is based on consumerism, commercialization, competition, and colonization, as we have seen, it becomes dangerous and unsustainable.

Political unrest: Governments today are often sophisticated tribal systems. Many countries are ruled by dictators and power-hungry individuals or small groups where, "if you had to kill them to protect your fellow tribesmen, you wasted no time on regret."

Today, we have clear demonstrations of this in countries such as Syria, Libya, Egypt, Central Africa, etc. The status quo of politics — dictatorships, corruption, power, and entrenched financial hierarchies — are on the defensive. Egypt, Libya, Syria, Oman, and other Middle Eastern countries are volatile. The facade that everything is OK, the main delusion people live with, is cracking.

We also see cracks in the United States government's "me first at all costs" leaders. Our elected representatives and many employed in the internal bureaucracy are pushed into extreme polarization. Lobbying organizations are focused on the success of their "part" and ignore the whole. The United States was facing down the "Occupy" movement in many cities using force, similar, but less lethal, than in other countries. The occupy protestors represented a potential threat to the status quo, as protestors in 1968 Chicago did.

The world's complex political systems, with their immense pressure to defend their part to survive, lie to each other and to the people they represent. It reminds me that after the Cold War, we discovered through actually talking to average Russian people that the real war had been between the two governments and not the people. The use of lies to create fear is the easiest way to control anyone. Again, this is nothing more than sophisticated tribal mentality.

Ecological factors: When Carl Sagan gave his prediction in 1977 that he felt we would reach an ecological tipping point within 50 years, it was very close. Buckminster Fuller, Paul R. Ehrlich, and others have also warned of the ecological damage the planet has sustained just since the Industrial Revolution.

The United Nations Environmental Programme (http://www.unep.org/themes/freshwater/) released a report in 2005 stating, "Fresh water will become the next planetary crisis." According to this report, at one point in the 1970s there was enough fresh water on the planet to give each person (if equally distributed) 7,000 cubic meters of fresh water. As of the year 2000 that number decreased to 4,000 cubic meters per person, per year, on the planet. In parts of the world such as the Horn of Africa, where drought is destroying the land and the people, there is less than 900 cubic meters of fresh water per person.

It is estimated that two out of every three people will live in water-stressed areas by the year 2025. In Africa alone, it is estimated that 25 countries will be experiencing water stress below 700 cubic meters Per capita per year by 2025. Today, 450 million people in 29 countries suffer from water shortages. (United Nations Environment Programme Assessment, 2005)

We also find reports from NASA, the World Health Organization, and the UN that severe water shortages affecting more than 400 million people today will affect 4 billion people by 2050.

These reports go on to say that half of all the world's coastal regions, where 1 billion people live, have degraded through overdevelopment or pollution and adequate sanitation facilities are lacking for those 2.4 billion people, meaning about 40 percent of the population will have ominous consequences.

A similar crisis is building with emissions and air pollution. We're all aware of the greenhouse effect of gasoline emissions, but a little-known and unpredicted occurrence could have even more disastrous effects. In 2007, an unusual Arctic fire along the tundra released a large amount of CO_2 into the atmosphere. Permafrost and tundra melts, in general, discharge enormous amounts of methane into the atmosphere causing even more greenhouse pressures.

Such fires are uncommon in the Arctic because the ground is normally covered with frost, snow, or ice. This may be changing according to the European Geosciences Union. They suggest that by 2016 Arctic summers may become snow and ice free. If 2005-2007 are indicators this prediction is actually closer than we think. The Arctic polar ice cap lost a record amount of ice cover during those years.

Nature magazine suggests that with Arctic warming speeding up, fires could become more common. Computer models failed to take into account these fires and other natural carbon events, such as the melting permafrost in Siberia. This is another potential ecological time bomb. More than a million square miles of peat bogs of the Siberian permafrost are melting. Beneath the sheet of frost is 2 trillion tons of methane gas, the equivalent of an entire century of fossil fuel carbon emissions.

As these carbon emissions affect the air, another crisis is threatening. Developed countries are using highly sophisticated technologies such as cell phones, computers, fax machines, printers, and other electronic devices that have the potential to create ecological crisis after crisis. In the U.S. the amount of electronic products being purchased is increasing at a staggering rate, maintains a 2006 Columbia University study. These products all use precious metals. Today companies are racing to mine all the precious metals they can find to meet the ever-increasing demand.

What many people don't know is that e-waste contains lead, mercury, and other toxins known to cause severe health problems in humans, particularly children. Correspondingly, dumping e-waste is another downside of our dependence on technology. E-waste is the fastest growing type of municipal solid waste in the U.S., and the dumping of e-waste that is having a devastating impact in Third World countries willing to take the waste. Many of these countries have already become the dumping grounds of electronic waste by the European Union, China, and the United States. Just outside of Ghana's biggest city, for example, smoke from smoldering e-waste spirals upward in the air above the Korle Lagoon, now one of the most polluted bodies of water on earth.

Weather: As we have seen, damage to Mother Earth through dumping and other toxic practices will be catastrophic in a few years and may have an effect even on the weather. We are seeing how the planet is reacting to our cancerous ways with increased numbers and intensity of hurricanes and tornados, earthquakes, drought, extreme heat, volcanic eruptions, and floods.

In a government report from Britain, published in August 2011, Paddy Ashdown, a member of the British House of Lords, said scientists believe recent natural disasters are not an aberration but "the beginnings of a new kind of future in which mega-disasters are going to be more frequent ... . The scale, frequency and severity of rapid onset humanitarian disasters will continue to grow in the coming years, and at an accelerating pace." According to the October 19, 2011, report from UNEP ("Trends in Natural Disasters"), "The statistics... reveal an exponential increase in disasters."

Are we too disconnected to care about all or any of this?

How We Became Disconnected

Don Miguel Ruiz, in his book *The Voice of Knowledge*, believes one of his favorite biblical legends could hold a key. He considers the story of the Garden of Eden the perfect mythical teaching of our disconnection.

Adam and Eve lived in harmony with nature, simply accepting "what is," the flow of life. When God gave Adam and Eve the power of choice so that, the legend says, "whoever eats the fruit of the Tree of Knowledge will have the knowledge of good and evil; they will know the difference between what is right and what is wrong, what is beautiful and what is ugly. They will gather all of that knowledge and begin to judge. Well, that is what happened in our head. And the symbolism of the apple is that every concept, every lie, is just like a fruit with a seed. When we place a fruit in fertile ground, the seed of the fruit creates another tree. That tree reproduces more fruit, and by the fruit, we know the tree."

This voice in our head, this dialogue (the fruit), is a phenomenon of the mind/brain, the Tree of Knowledge. This observable fact brings with it a sense of separation from everything else. Because everything becomes an object of observation. Therefore, I am separate!

(Ironically this very phenomenon can bring us back to our true essence. When we question who is listening to this inner voice or I am not what I can perceive we come to realize our essence.)

When you and I became old enough to learn language, we also took a bite from the deceptive fruit and opened ourselves to the voice of judgments: "The world is imperfect" and "There isn't enough in life," for example. Eventually, we turned this voice upon ourselves. The lie of "perfectionism" or "not being enough" or "I can't" pollutes our thoughts and finally we disconnect by closing our spiritual eye.

Eventually, our spiritual blindness at an early age requires the structure of certainty and safety. In order to achieve this, we turn to our internal dialogue and the voice pointing us to the world outside of ourselves. But this also creates suffering.

Sure, most of these mental conversations are the beliefs people, such as parents, grandparents, teachers, ministers, and early caregivers passed on to you. This becomes your neurological programming. Of course, you had to accept their "truth" because who else would you trust? You believed whatever was told to you, and this began the way you viewed the world. In scientific terms, your senses delivered information to "mirror neurons" from watching your mother, father, siblings, and, the outer world. This also creates a sense of separation that causes you to doubt your inner connection for no other reason than it conflicts with the beliefs you were told and saw as a child.

From this experience, your inner storyteller, the voice in your head, developed a story. But the story is not the reality. It is a virtual world like a show on TV. It appears real, but it's just a representation.

What would happen if you were watching this TV show, especially on a big screen, and all your senses become completely engaged? I mean you became so absorbed in it that you saw, heard, felt, and experience what's on the screen.

What happens is you initially hear your internal dialogue talking about the show. Then your internal conversations give way and your thoughts and feelings become part of the show. As your feelings are triggered, you finally pay no attention to what is around you, in fact, you pay no attention to anything outside of the TV. Your onscreen lover is about to arrive and you get excited. Or, someone is walking into a trap and you scream for them stop.

You might say you were "caught up" in the TV show. Your attention was so absorbed it became "your reality." This is basically how most people live their lives. The great Eastern masters call this the "trance of life." We live in a trance with our spiritual eye closed, mistaking our perceptions of reality for reality.

On several occasions as a child I had out-of-body experiences. At some unknown point I would move to the top corner of the room and watch the scene as it played before me. It was the same when I had a near-death experience. It began as flash and my awareness moved to the corner of the room observing. Is life just another TV show?

How Did We Get Here?

The goddesses worldview of 10,000 years ago recognized that every aspect of creation was sacred. Similar to many indigenous tribes. During the past 5,000 years male gods started taking over goddess based cultures. This shifted scriptures and worldview based on a male creator separate from "His" creation.

AS a result, prior to the 17th century, science was under the control of and part of the domain of religion—meant to prove religious dogma of a male viewpoint. Those who practiced "science" were called natural philosophers, as there was no concept of a scientist. At that time, an important paradigm shift took place, and three great scientists propagated a theory that became the standard for philosophy and religion.

Galileo, Sir Issac Newton, and Giordano Bruno, at different times, all believed the world was a giant machine. This "threesome of science" laid the foundations for the theory known as classical mechanics, which demonstrated universal gravitation, the three laws of motion, the rotation of stars in a galaxy, and the revolution of planets around suns—all mechanical processes.

So, if the universe is mechanical, and we are part of the universe, then by deduction what interpretation must be made about who we are? We, humans, are machines.

Four centuries later, the mechanistic viewpoint persists. The medical profession looks at the body and its parts as a machine. If something is wrong with an organ, for example, a specialist for that part takes it out and replaces it, whether it be a hip, a heart, a stomach, part of the brain, even systems such as the endocrine system. Each specialist knows about a particular part and how to fix or replace it. When you go to the doctor with your problem, most often they send you to a specialist, then a different specialist, and no one has the bigger, whole picture. The result is that healing is actually fixing.

We lost something profound with the threesome's theory of the mechanical universe. Foremost is our sense of connection: connection to the transcendent, to the universe, to the earth, to one another, and to our own souls.

How to Reconnect

We have considered the part disconnection plays in today's problems in order to know the root cause of our suffering. However, reconnecting is not easy. We all tend to avoid our inner lives. Some of us are fearful of this inner world. Others are busy, and not everybody has the time or the inclination to undertake such a sensitive task as reconnecting. Yet we owe it to everyone to stop ours and the collective ego's destructive ways. But we need help.

Two areas are vital in reconnecting: the mind and the heart.

Mind: The first phase to reconnecting is to understand our internal dialogue. We now know the voice in our head, the one saying, "You are wrong," "you are ugly," "you are not enough," "you are … they are," is the untrained mind, and it means we can do something about it. As Don Miguel Ruiz and Byron Katie both suggest, we need to start questioning our thoughts. Is this thought true? How do you know it's true? And my favorite: Who is the you who is listening to this voice?

Heart: Earlier I quoted Nisargaddata Maharaj, the Hindu mystic, who said, "There is the material world and the spiritual. Between lies the universal mind and universal heart. It is wise love that makes the two one."

Based on that quote, we have given far more attention to the mind than to the heart. Although the heart has been relegated to the position of 'romantic,' studies in the science of the heart have measured a toroidal electromagnetic energy field (Sonya Kim, Heartmath Institute) directly centered in the heart.

While you were in science class you most likely saw a demonstration of the pattern of a magnetic field when your teacher placed a magnet under a sheet of paper and sprinkled iron filings onto the top of the sheet of paper. This pattern is the result of an EM field.

The EM field of the heart is the center of energy communications. Even though in our modern society we are very advanced we have problems accepting that the heart receives information. The first issues is that the rational part of us ignores most of the information from the heart because it doesn't come to us as we normally want it to, that is, through verbal thought. Usually it arrives as intuition. Also, we are so energetically closed down that amazing amounts of energy come into our system and are trapped in the heart causing communication blocks.

The heart actually does think, although not the same way that the mind/brain verbally does, but like the subconscious mind, quietly.

The heart has cells and neurological structure similar to, comparable with, and in communication with, the brain's neuro-structure. A direct connection comes from the heart, goes through the ganglia, up the spine and into what are called glial cells around the brain's hemispheres. In the past the glial cells were called gray matter, or the packing material or glue for the brain. Turns out, these cells are a large neural network of billions of cells. What that means is the information coming from the heart enters into the cells of the brain, believed to be predominately the right hemisphere. "Thinking" by the heart is called intuition.

The Aboriginal people of Australia, a 40,000- or 50,000-year-old culture, marvel at people like you and I because we think in words, they don't. They think in the same way babies think, or as the Buddhists would say, "no mind," blank. Information comes to them and flows through them into actions. Rarely did they go through conscious, rational thought processes until the late 1700's, when Britain decided to settle Australia as a penal colony.

Typical of tribal mentality the British decided to eradicate the indigenous culture—much as was done with the Native American Indian after the settlers arrived.

The Aboriginal culture was much more heart centric and in harmony with Nature. A wonderful example of this is that they can tell you where any other member of their tribe is located. They can find fresh water under the desert floor without anything except their knowing. They can tell where it's going to rain and when—so they can be there before it happens.

If you ask them how, their response is blank because they don't rationalize and think through a process of finding out where it's going to rain or watch CNN weather to find out. They have their own information, and it comes from their heart.

So the heart, is an amazing organ, tool and spiritual environment. And, as many of the sacred traditions suggest, it represents the universal principles of love and altruism—the giving of individuals and Spirit.

Reconnection is about our relationship to our heart. The heart receives EM impulses and information from our own internal system and from the environment. Modern cultures have lost touch with this critically important part of what it means to be human.

For most of us we take in the information and resist it or block it. But that energy doesn't go away. It remains blocked circulating in a narrow space around the heart. Since the major contributor to death in modern countries is heart disease perhaps we should reexamine the importance of the heart energy system.

For you and I, we can begin to reconnect by letting go of the resistance we hold in our heart. In my early twenties I fell in love and discovered the power of love. We walked the beaches of Southern California and talked for hours about all the things going on in life.

Then she found a religion that wouldn't permit her to talk or be around anyone outside their group. She let me go. This was one of my first lesson in the darkness of the heart.

At first everything was just black. My eyes only saw a darkness, I even experienced palpations, heart pain, and loss of appetite. As time went on I carried around a heaviness in my chest and drug myself around like a beaten victim.

In retrospect I recognize the heaviness as my heart field being shut down. For a long time this exhibited as barking at co-workers, and stayed inside my sadness/anger grief until a healer friend helped me realize the original loss had now morphed into a universal loss because my heart was locked.

Like many of us at first, I was completely resistant to this process. But, she talked to me about my pain, and walked me through it. As I began her process I was sure I would die, the darkness seem to increase. Then as I completed the process a lightness came over me like a fresh summer rain shower and my initial skepticism gave way to relief.

As I experience, the demands of letting go seem so daunting yet it turned out to be much less painful than the ego believed and much less than the chronic state of pain I was experiencing.

That said, let me introduce you to the process that she took me through all those years ago. Breathing is the first element to letting blocked energy go. I sat quietly and watch my breath. After five or ten minutes focus awareness on my heart I notice heaviness in my chest. She told me to breath into the heaviness until it becomes lighter. After some time she said repeat this process till your heart felt lighter. The tears faded and life was lighter. I also learned in that process to let go and not to resist life, and I saw how addicted to our egotism we are.

The heart field is powerful but our head/mind is also responsible for our dilemma. In this area you have to start questioning your thoughts.

Is this thought true? How do I know that it is true? Question every thought until you begin to awaken to the truth. Most of your dialogue is lies, untruths that are just another part of the programming created by your early life.

We are so often the cause of our misery. We want and pursue people and things we know in our hearts are not going to give us the happiness we want or the relief from troubles we desire. Letting go, or nonresistance, is the first step to shifting your life!

Background for Shifting Consciousness

We have considered the importance of reconnecting with our true Selves as the basis for the next step shifting our consciousness. Heaven on Earth is truly about living as spiritual beings with all the values and understanding this implies. So, we must move from the old conquest, competition, colonization, and consumerism paradigms to a world that is collaborative, connected, conscious, and intuitive.

The following definitions will help us make this shift.

Ego: the sense that I exist as a separate being. When the body breathes, the mind says, "I am breathing." Egos like labels, having a name for example, Larry, Marigene, etc. Whereas Mind is very daring, ego is very much afraid.

Mind: a tool of consciousness and our individual use of the Universal Mind.

Universal Mind: As far back in history as we have records, questions of the underlying nature of the

Universe have been asked, explored, and investigated. Through time we can see the maturity of science as it discarded one idea for another and changed as its understanding of other parts of science changed. The quests continue today.

Early philosophers, for instance, speculated the primary element in the universe was water. However, in ancient Greece it was widely accepted that the four basic elements of everything were earth, air, water, and fire. As we travel through time, we see these theories change and center around chemical elements, then microscopic building blocks, then molecular structure, atomic elements, and so on. In recent years, speculation from some of the foremost thinkers of quantum physics has shifted the concept of the fundamental building blocks of the universe again.

Daniel J. Chalmers and a number of other contemporary physicists consider *information* the fundamental element. In one of his papers, Chalmers states:

[Physicist John Archibald] Wheeler (1990) has suggested that information is fundamental to the physics of the universe. According to this 'it from bit' doctrine, the laws of physics can be cast in terms of information, postulating different states that gave rise to different issues without actually saying what those states are. It is only their position in an information space that counts. *(International Journal of Theoretical Physics,* 42)

Philosophically people have had various names for Universal Mind: Rudolf Steiner's concept of *higher worlds*, Carl Jung's *collective unconscious*, Ernest Holmes' *race mind*, Karl Pribram's *frequency spectrum*, Jesus' *spirit of wholeness*, *The Mind of God*, the *Akashic record* . These are all names for this cosmological information field. Untold billions of thoughts and actions, positive, negative, or neutral, have fed this field over vast periods of time.

The notion of Universal Mind came into the Western canon in Athens during the pre-Socratic time around 480 B.C. Philosopher Anaxagoras became known as Nous or Mind, because he taught that "all things" were created by Mind and that Mind held the cosmos together. This he considered the connection to the cosmos for human beings, a pathway to the divine.

According to this Nous concept, Universal Mind is:

omniscient (all-knowing)

omnipotent (all-powerful)

omnificent (all-creative)

omnipresent (always now).

Metaphorically, Universal Mind is like the data the Internet is accessing. To you and I this information is somewhere. Where we are not sure, but through the Internet we have access to it. Intuition, like the Internet, is our access to Universal Mind.

Our local mind stores thoughts, actions, emotions, associations, and perceptions in what we now call our mind/body field. All of these records are constantly updated locally and universally. Again using the metaphor of the personal computer this storage is Random Access Memory (RAM). Access is through our brain's interconnected neural networks.

Everyone has access to Universal Mind, unlike the Internet; the infrastructure for us is hardwired. Edgar Casey, the famous psychic, and hundreds of thousands of others have discovered this access. You have it too; you just aren't aware of it. Many of the thoughts that randomly pour through your mind are part of this Universal Mind. If we have a strong thought, coupled with emotion, the energy of that thought will bring similar thoughts to your mind. These similar thoughts come from Universal Mind.

Before anything can be created, a thought must trigger the creative process. Thought and feeling are the key ingredients of creating. Your thought is a product of your local mind and feeds Universal Mind, the creative seat from which all proceeds. Our local mind forms the thought, and Universal Mind fills the thought with particular energy to create form.

But it requires "charged" thought, meaning thought accompanied by feeling. Thought and feeling together are the mold. Thought without feeling is a mold without depth.

It could be roughly compared to 3D printing. This process takes a one-dimensional plan or drawing and converts it into a three-dimensional mold using a layering process. The mold is then filled with say plaster and the end result is created.

You are, today, the result of all of yesterday's thoughts. Tomorrow you shall be the result of what you are now thinking plus all of the yesterdays'. Human beings create their own ego character, personality, and environment by the thoughts they originate, organize, and hold as beliefs.

In the work I am suggesting we are creating a "mold" for the betterment of humanity. I also call this process "seeding consciousness." You are, in fact, combining an inner experience of thought, image, feeling, memory, associations, and perception to create the mold. You must have the thought, image, feeling, associations and the internal "virtual experience" of what you want to create or nothing happens.

Think about this: Most of us think about what we don't want all day long. We know what the experience will be if it happens; we often see the whole movie of this experience, in our mind, and have strong feelings about not wanting it. Usually at some point the negative experience manifests, and we say, "That's just what I expected." The process works either way; we just aren't as practiced in using it for positive experience.

To shift the collective, then, we must seed Universal Mind with the crystal clarity of our thought/feeling. Our purpose in shifting the collective consciousness is to create peace and harmony for the collective.

The Future of the Future (background)

The Future of the Future is about creating. It is a manifestation process based on ancient wisdom and supported by new science.

There are four concepts that help explain this process: l) the memory-prediction framework, 2) imagination as real, 3) emotion in recall, and 4) the past as certain.

1) *Memory-prediction framework:* This first theory is hypothesized by Jeff Hawkins in his book *On Intelligence*. This theory relates the brain's ability to match sensory input with stored memory patterns and the follow on process that leads to predictions of what will happen in the future. Hawkins describes the various brain parts that play a role in this process: the mammalian neocortex, our most complex organ, which plays an indispensable role in many human behaviors; the hippocampus, the part of the brain that is involved in memory forming, organizing, and storing; and the thalamus, which is involved in sensory perception and regulation of motor functions.

With these parts working together, the brain will process information from the senses and pass it up to other areas of the brain to essentially predict a future outcome. As such, the brain is a feed-forward hierarchical system that predicts the future from past data. This system worked well in pre-history survival scenarios but evolution has not kept up with the advances in the world.

2) *Imagination as real:* During this step we expand our horizon in this process to include imagination. If you imagine an action in your mind, parts of your brain act as if it is an actual event. Neuroscientist Michael Gazzaniga, discusses a study in the *Journal of Neuroscience*, that suggest why this happens, "In humans there are mirror neurons that correspond to movements all over the body, and they fire even when there is no goal; in fact, the same neurons are active even when we only imagine an action. Therefore if you imagine an action your mirror neurons believe it to be an actual event." Mirror neurons also grasp emotions. Thus imagined emotions are treated as part of actual event by the mirror neurons. This brain mechanism gives us an ability to experience an event in our imagination as if it were actually taking place.

3) *Emotion in recall:* Emotion plays a strong part in memory recall. When Candace Pert, the Chief of the Section on Brain Biochemistry of the Clinical Neuroscience Branch of the National Institutes of Health, began her studies on peptides, receptors, and the role of these neuropeptides, she found evidence that memory occurs at the point of synapse in the neurons. She says, "The sensitivity of the receptors are part of memory and pattern storage. But the peptide network extends beyond the hippocampus, to organs, tissue, skin, muscle and endocrine glands. They all have peptides receptors on them and can access and store emotional information. This means the emotional memory is stored in many places in the body, not just the brain."

The stronger the emotion, the easier the access. If we couple this with the concept that everything at its fundamental level is vibration, then a thought(s) coupled with emotion has a stronger vibration than thought alone.

In our process we can take a stored emotion from another event and attach it to our imagined event. By imagining a event in the future and attaching a desired emotion we set the stage for manifestation.

4) ***Past as certain****:* Studies have found that memories are thoughts, emotions, perceptions, associations, and images held in the mind as "certain." Given that memories are always about an earlier period, they are represented in our mind as done and therefore certain. Bring up a memory and you will notice how certain it feels. We treat them as a certainty compared to the future which we treat as uncertain.

Taken together these four concepts are the explanation for how memory, strongly held with emotion, creates part of our outer reality and can be used to shift your reality.

With this background as preparation be open and receptive to the "magic" of this process. If you are open, it says you've let go of your energy blocks.

Staying open is a matter if nonresistance, acceptance or surrender. Allow energy to pass through you. Watch it and notice it as it flows. Resistance blocks the flow. Let yourself go to the experience.

The Future of the Future Process

Let's go through the steps in the process.

1) State or write your intention, like a screenplay.

a) In this first step you must determine the "what." What do you want to experience? You need to be clear on what you want. The more specific you are, the easier it is to imagine.

For example, when you go to an online store's order page, you already have in mind what you want. As you fill in the web form, you have to fill in the particulars of what you want. You cannot leave the product field empty. The web page will not allow you to place an empty order. The computer page will likely reply, "Please enter the product desired." Clearly, you have to be specific on what you want.

b) When you know what you want to experience, *write it down*. One of the suggestions in goal-setting classes is to write your goal down. As you become clear on what you want, fill in the additional information, such as the characters in the scene, and develop the details into a movie screenplay. What does the environment look like? Who is in the scene? What are the colors? The feelings? Other details?

c) Imbue the scene with emotion. Recall a scene from your past in which you experienced similar qualities and emotions to what you want to experience in this movie. For example, if you want to experience joy, recall a memory that has joy in it.

2) Step into the movie.

Now I want you to stand up (if you are not already standing), eyes closed. Take a step forward into your movie and begin nodding your head, as if you are saying yes. You are now in the movie, where your intention has become an actual real event, right now.

Your current reality is the movie from Step 1. Describe the scene out loud to yourself as if it is happening now. Make sure you are in the scene and you are seeing everything before you through your eyes. Move yourself through the movie and the environment and events just as you wrote them down. See and hear the people through your eyes and ears. Physically move around in this scene, perhaps down a street or through a room—carefully, while keeping your eyes closed.

Once the movie is complete, blank the movie screen in your imagination and continue to Step 3.

3) Step into the future and look back.

Continuing with your eyes closed, take another step into the future, physically beyond where you stood in Step 2 when you were describing the current reality.

You have moved into the future, so you can now look back and into the past because your movie has already happened. Now describe the experience of the scene in Step 2, in past tense, knowing it is already past. Notice your feelings that it must be real because it is now in the past. All you wanted to create has happened!

Carry this knowing with you from moment to moment and day to day, and you will soon see what you didn't before.

Seeding Planetary Shift

On the next page is an example of seeding planetary change.

1) State or write your intention, like a screenplay.

What positive outcome do we want for the planet?

See a movie, in color and with sound, of the whole planet of beings living and working in harmony with each other and nature. See and hear the people. See nature as pleasant, supportive, and creative.

Also, notice the size of the movie. If it is far away or small, bring it closer or make it larger.

Write the screenplay of this movie. What does the environment look like? Who is in the scene? What are the colors? The feelings? Other details? Make sure you are in the scene and you are seeing everything before you through your eyes. This event is happening *now*.

2) Step into the movie.

Now, I want you to stand up (if you are not already standing), eyes closed. Take a step forward and into the movie.

Visualize the movie scene in your imagination as if it were taking place right now. See the whole planet of beings living and working in harmony with each other and nature. See and hear the people.

When the movie is complete, blank the screen in your mind and move to Step 3.

3) Step into the future and look back.

Continuing with your eyes closed, step into the future.

Now look back at your completed movie; you are looking into the past. Describe the original movie as though it is past. In other words, you're looking at this past scene of the whole planet of beings as they lived and worked in harmony with each other and nature.

Describe the scene as if you are telling a reporter what took place.

Notice your feelings that it must be real because it is now past. It happened!

Carry this knowing with you from moment to moment and day to day, and you will soon see what you didn't before—the whole planet of beings living and working in harmony with each other and nature.

Alan Wolf, a quantum physicist scientist, hit on this theme in his book *Parallel Universes,* writing, " The fact that the future may play a role in the present is a new prediction of the mathematical laws of quantum physics. If interpreted literally, the mathematical formulas indicate ... how the future enters our present. ..."

The process in action

I was developing this process (in an evolutionary way) in the mid 1990s, and here is how it unfolded. When I completed a position in Seattle, Washington, my wife, Marigene, and I moved to St. Louis to take care of her aging mother.

I began writing down what I wanted to create for my next job. At some point, having written screenplays before, I decided to write up my vision as one. That meant having a storyline, characters, plot, settings, etc.—a full-blown story.

Visualization and imagination have always been important to me, leading me to screenwriting in the first place, so upon completion of this screenplay, I decided to begin visualizing it as a movie.

In my script I was sitting and working in an office with large windows looking out over a grassy area. There were people coming and going from this rather large office and writings on whiteboards. Many discussions were happening before, during, and after hours. I also imagined how much I was making per year and the various benefits that came with the job. My intention for the work was always one of helping people realize the truth of who they are.

Over a period of several weeks I ran the screenplay in my imagination. In the meantime my wife and mother-in-law wanted to travel to Hawaii and stay for a month with a friend on the island of Maui.

Reluctantly (not because I didn't want to go to Hawaii, but because I wanted to work on the process), I agreed and we set off for Maui. The flight is a perfect time, I thought, to continue to do the work of imagining. Here was a six-hour block of time when I couldn't go anywhere but the plane.

Once we landed and got settled, I began working on the movie of my mind. Even after we had been on the island for two weeks I was still giving an hour or two a day to the process. Some days I sat near the pool that looked out over the Four Seasons Hotel to the blue waters of the ocean. If knew if I could stay completely focused on my imagination movie then I had trained myself pretty well. And it did take training, just like sitting for meditation.

One day I sat in the early morning darkness and a warm ocean breeze touched my face. I opened my eyes, and for some reason I couldn't get back into imaging. After several days of this I said to Marigene, "I can't focus on the screenplay anymore. I don't know why."

Casually, she said, "That's because it is different now!"

I don't know why, but that word "now" provoked a shift in my imagining the screenplay from it happening in the future to it taking place in the present. This meant I should imagine the movie as a participant in it, not watching it as a spectator.

Within a week the same thing happened again. I could no longer imagine the movie. This time, I remembered Ernest Holmes writing in his *Science of Mind* textbook, and in *Creative Mind and Success*,

"You have to know it is done." The inevitable struggle between my rational and intuitive minds had began.

So I kicked this concept around: "Done." My mind would say, "There is nothing you imagined in front of you, is there? So you are fooling yourself."

Even though I knew better from all my New Thought studies, I was having trouble with "done."

Then I heard a voice say, "It's a memory."

That was it! I could easily look back at the movie as a memory and say to it's done because I had a memory of it. There was no doubt about it.

Much to my dismay, we then traveled from Maui to Seattle to visit our kids. I wanted to get home and wait for the telephone call from this new job.

Having learned not to resist, however, we arrived at our daughter's house near Bellingham, Washington. Everyone was hungry and wanted to go out to dinner. Well, not everyone. I felt I needed to stay—don't know why—so I did.

Shortly after they left for dinner, my daughter's phone rang and the voice on the other end asked for Larry. Now, no one knew where I was (and there were no ubiquitous cell phones). I said, "Yes, this is Larry."

"Mr. De Rusha, I got your number from your application that Jerry, another head hunter friend, had on file. I hope it is all right to call you here. I know this is the emergency contact number on the application."

The long and short of it is that a company in Beverton, Oregon, was looking for someone and I was the someone who qualified. However, the project they wanted me for wasn't starting for a month, but they were willing to pay me for a month to stay available.

When I agreed to the position, I received everything that was in my screenplay—including the large office with large windows. Turns out they didn't have any more offices available and they offered me the conference room.

Remember my intention to help people? In my job I would go into the office/conference room early and people would stop by and ask who I was and what I was doing. Inevitably the conversation would turn to why they hired me so early and I would describe my story.

For more than a month I had groups of people who would come to work early and stay late to listen to my talking about metaphysics.

This was the point at which The Future of The Future was born, though I didn't know what to call it then.

I used the process again nine months later and became the chief operating officer of a venture capital company.

The Challenge

It would seems that quantum physics has given us proof of the Biblical statement, "I have said, 'Ye are gods; and all of you are children of the Most High' " Psalms, and John's New Testament statement, "I and the Father are one."

You might take issue with this proof from science, as I did. First, it moves God out of the realm of super-being to the "ground of being" or "downward causation." Second, it becomes an impersonal principle or law. These are not new concepts, as they appear in many sacred texts, but never before has science said, "God is all!"

There are two types of causation: upward and downward. In the world that views life as an upward causality chain, it begins with subatomic particles causing atoms, which cause molecules, cells, organs, all the way up to the brain causing the mind and consciousness. In this view all is created from the bottom up, through upward interactions and by matter being manipulated.

Downward causation is the reverse and begins with consciousness as the "ground of being." In consciousness all are possibilities. Therefore, everything comes from consciousness. You are not the mind and body, since these are perceivable, what you can perceive you are not. You are the observer. This means you influence the wave of possibility and thus create as a god does.

I support that each person is a god, from a quantum consciousness standpoint.

I also support that there are many forces that do not want the population of the world to know this and thus overturn their negative use of this power. In 1994 a neurophysiologist, Jose Grinberg-Zylberbaum, disappeared (presumed kidnapped) because he was on the way to proving his theory of nonlocality experimentally. Since then, more than four experiments have proved this theory to be a fact. Amit Goswami, Ph.D. a theoretical physicist continued the work and succeeded in verifying the formulas.

Since time began, people who have made this discovery and tried to release it to the general public in a way people could understand have died (Jesus, for one) or disappeared. In some cases funding has been cut off for departments or schools supporting this work. Yet, other people are not the only object in our way.

On the local level we are all subject to conditioning; that is, the constant drone of what other people believe. These beliefs become part of our programming. The beliefs of our parents, teachers, church, and the like pattern the neuronal structure of our memories and beliefs.

This raises the question of how to overcome the programming. There are some techniques in psychology and neuroscience to help, but the best way is to go beyond the mind and its programming to the higher levesl of consciousness. This is what all the great traditions have said we must do, but they are not clear on the how. Most frequently, the process is meditation, which provides entrainment of the brain/mind with higher levels of consciousness and provides contact with possibilities.

The central premise of this book—that any global shift begins with you—means you have to work first on reconnecting to your spiritual essence. Use mediation, prayer, contemplation, and any of the other tools of the many great spiritual traditions. Such reconnection is demonstrated by your renewed sense of compassion for yourself and others and by your willingness to let go of the old paradigm that creates suffering.

As you cultivate compassion and inner peace for yourself, you then move to another level of consciousness—compassion at the level of humanity, the planet, and the cosmos at large. Let go of your conditioned mental and emotional patterns that trap you and limit the flow of your authentic Self.

When the world begins to move ever faster toward its new paradigm, chaos will become more dramatic. Humanity's future for the next few decades may be rocky and distressing. That which is out of balance cannot be sustained—it will end one way or the other.

As a part of this race consciousness called humanity, you may experience difficulty as well, though this will be influenced by the degree to which you have been able to reconnect and stay with your inner peace. By staying out of the drama of change and focusing more on peace and clarity in your own mind and heart, by staying compassionate throughout any changes, you will be doing the work needed for positive change. Remember that this is all some drama of a universe we have yet to comprehend. Amit Goswami says in Quantum Activism, "My conclusion: the only viable technique available to us right now to deal with the tyranny of negative emotions is to balance them with the production of positive emotional brain circuits.

This is what our journey of transformation is largely about."

The Future of the Future process can help shape this new paradigm. With your help and the help of all other compassionate beings, we can affect this positive change.

In addition to this, there are other, countless, ways to help: learning and teaching compassion, forgiving others, learning about diet and how it affects you and the planet, practicing meditation and other sacred techniques, and letting go of your attachment to material goods—in other words, simplifying your life.

Now is the time to get connected. Begin to shift consciousness by seeding your garden of consciousness so that in a month, a year, two years, or three years, the reports from the world garden will also be magnificent.

Suggested Reading

An Inconvenient Truth: The Planetary Emergency of Global Warming and What We Can Do About It. Gore, Al. 2007, Emmaus, PA.: Rodale Press.

Biology of Transcendence, Joseph Chilton Pearce, 2010. New York: Park Street Press.

Common Wealth: Economics for a Crowded Planet. Sachs, Jeffrey. 2008. New York: Penguin.

Cosmos and Psyche: Intimations of a New World View. Tarnas, Richard. London: Viking UK.

Death of Religion and Rebirth of Spirit, Joseph Chilton Pearce, 2011. New York:Park Street Press.

Entangled Minds, Extrasensory Experiences in Quantum Reality. Dean Radin. 2008. New York: Paraview Pocket Books.

Fabric of the Cosmos, Brian Green. 2010. New York: Vintage Press.

Global Shift, Edmund J. Bourne, 2007. Noetic Books, New Harbinger.

Hot, Flat, and Crowded. Friedman, Thomas L. 2008. New York: Farrar, Straus & Giroux.

Radical Nature: Rediscovering the Soul of Matter. de Quincey, Christian. 2008. Montpelier, VT.: Invisible Cities Press.

Science and the Akashic Field: An Integral Theory of Everything. Laszlo, Ervin. Rochester, VT.: Inner Traditions.

Self-Aware Universe: How Consciousness Creates the Material World. Amit Goswani, New York: Tarcher/Putnam.

The Living Universe. Elgin, Duane. San Francisco, CA: Berrett-Koehler Publishers

Toward a Theory of Consciousness, by David Chalmers Cambridge, MA: MIT, Press.

Quantum Healing. New York: Bantam-Doubleday. Deepak Chopra, D.

Quantum Shift in the Global Brain, Ervin Laszlo, Inner Traditions.

Voice of Knowledge. Ruiz, Don Miguel, Amber-Allen Publishing.

Waking the Global Heart. Judith, Anodea. Santa Rosa, CA: Elite -Books.

WorldShift 2012: Making Green Business, New Politics, and Higher Consciousness Work Together. Ervin Laszlo, Inner Traditions.

Vibrational Medicine: The #1 Handbook of Subtle-Energy Therapies. Rochester, VT.Bear & Company.

Websites

www.planetaryshift.org

www.secretofknowing.com

www.worldshift.org

www.scienceofspirit.org

www.quantumactivist.com/invitation

Center for Conscious Evolution (evolve.org)

DavidKorten.org (davidkorten.org)

Emergent Mind (emergentmind.org)

Global Community (globalcommunity.org)

Institute of Noetic Sciences (noetic.org)

Kosmos Journal (kosmosjournal.org)

WiserEarth (wiserearth.org)

Biblography

Assagioli, Roberto. Psychosynthesis.(1971): Viking Press.

Bard, Arthur S., M.D., and Mitchell G. Bard, Ph.D., (2002). The Complete Idiot's Guide to Understanding the Brain. New York: Alpha.

Bateson, G. (1980). Mind and Nature. New York: Bantam.

Behe, M. J. (1996). Darwin's Black Box. New York: Simon & Schuster.

Begley, Sharon. (2007). Train Your Mind, Change Your Brain: How a New Science Reveals Our Extraordinary Potential to Transform Ourselves. New York: Ballantine Books

Bell, J. S. (1965). "On the Einstein, Podolsky, Rosen paradox." Physics, vol. 1, pp. 195-200.

Blood, C. (1993). "On the Relation of the mathematics of quantum mechanics to the perceived physical universe and free will." Preprint. Camden, NJ: Rutgers University.

Bohm, David. (1996). Wholeness and The Implicate Order. London: Routledge.

Capra, Fritjof, Ph.D. (1997). Thinking Allowed. Thinking Allowed Productions.

Chalmers, D. (1995). Toward a Theory of Consciousness. Cambridge, MA: MIT Press.

Chopra, D. (1990). Quantum Healing. New York: Bantam-Doubleday.

Cohen, A., and Wilber, K. (2009). "The second face of God." EnlightenNext,

Critchley, H. D., Daly, E. M., Bullmore, E. T., Williams, S. C. R., Van Amelsvoort, T., Robertson, D. M., Rowe, A., Phillips, M., McAlonan, G., Howlin, P., and Murphy, D.G. (2000). The functional neuroanatomy of social behavior: Changes in cerebral blood flow when people with autistic disorder process facial expressions. Brain 123, 2203–2212.

de Quincey, Christian. (2008). Deep Spirit. The Wisdom Academy Press; thewisdomacademy.org

DeRusha, Laurence. (2010) The Secret of Knowing: The Science of Intuition, Amazon;CreateSpace.

Dossey, Larry, M.D. (1982) Space, Time and Medicine, fifth edition. Boston: Shambhala Publications .

Estés, Clarissa Pinkola, Ph.D. (2009). Mother Night: Myths, Stories, and Teachings for Learning to See in the Dark. Sounds True, Inc.

Gazzaniga, Michael. S. (2004). The Cognitive Neurosciences III. Boston: MIT Press.

Gladwell, Malcolm. (2007) Blink: The Power of Thinking Without Thinking. New York: Back Bay Books.

Goswami, Amit. (2011). How Quantum Activism Can Save Civilization: A Few People Can Change Human Evolution, Hampton Roads, Kindle Edition.

Holmes, Ernest. S. (1932). Science of Mind. Los Angeles: McBride & Sons.

Jenkins, W. M., and M. M. Merzenich, M. T. Ochs, T. Allard, and E. Guic-Robles. (1990) "Functional Reorganization of Primary Somatosensory Cortex in Adult Owl Monkeys after Behavioral Controlled Tactile Stimulation." Journal of Neurophysiology, Vol. 63, Issue 1

Kaku, Michio. (2009) The Physics of the Impossible. New York: Anchor

Khan, Pir Vilayat Inayat. (2000) Awakening, A Sufi Experience, Taarcher edition.

Karpinski, Gloria. (1990). Where Two Worlds Touch: Spiritual Rites of Passage. New York: Ballantine Books.

Klein, Gary A. (1999). The Sources of Power—How People Make Decisions. Boston: MIT Press.

Laszlo, Ervin. (2007). Science and the Akashic Field—An Integral Theory of Everything. Rochester, Vermont: Inner Traditions.

McCraty, R., M. Atkinson, and R. T. Bradley. (2004) "Electrophysiological Evidence of Intuition: Part 2. A System-Wide Process." Institute for Whole Social Science and Institute of HeartMath. The Journal of

Alternative and Complementary Medicine, Vol. 10, No. 2

McFadden, Johnjoe. (2009). "The Conscious Electromagnetic Field Theory." Surrey, England. www.surrey.ac.uk/qe/cemi.htm.

McTaggart, Lynne. (2008). The Field: The Quest for the Secret Force of the Universe. New York: Harper Paperbacks.

Myss, Caroline, Ph.D. Anatomy of the Spirit: The Seven Stages of Power and Healing. New York: Three Rivers Press (1997)

New World Encyclopedia. (2010) http://www.newworldencyclopedia.org/entry/Paul_Broca

Orloff, Judith, M.D. (2004). Positive Energy: 10 Extraordinary Prescriptions for Transforming Fatigue, Stress, and Fear into Vibrance, Strength & Love. Harmony Press

Ornstein, Robert. (1991). The Evolution of Consciousness: Of Darwin, Freud, and Cranial Fire:

The Origins of the Way We Think. New York: Simon & Schuster

Pinker, Steven. (2009) How the Mind Works. New York: W.W. Norton & Company.

Pottenger, James P., Ph.D. (2010). Holographic Psychology: The Science of Spirit. San Diego: Community Church of Religious Science.

Pribram, Karl H. (1971). Languages of the Brain: Experimental Paradoxes and Principles of Neuropsychology. New York: Prentice-Hall

Ruiz, Don Miguel (2011-07-07). The Voice of Knowledge, Amber-Allen Publishing. Kindle Edition.

Russell, Peter. (2009). "The Primacy of Consciousness."
http://www.peterrussell.com/SP/PrimConsc.php

Sarbin, Theodore. (1960). Clinical Inference and Cognitive Theory. New York: Holt, Rinehart & Winston.

Schwartz, Jeffrey M., M.D., and Sharon Begley. (2003) The Mind and the Brain: Neuroplasticity and the

Power of Mental Force. San Francisco: Harper Perennial.

Siegfried, T. (2000). The Bit and the Pendulum: From Quantum Computing to M Theory-The New Physics of Information. New York: John Wiley & Sons;

Targ, Russell, Ph.D. (2004) Limitless Mind: A Guide to Remote Viewing and Transformation of Consciousness. Novato, California: New World Library.

Wheeler, J. A. (1990). Information, physics, quantum: the search for links. In: Zurek W. H., ed. Complexity, Entropy, and the Physics of Information. Santa Fe Institute Studies in the Sciences of Complexity, vol. VIII.Reading, Massachusetts: Perseus Books

Wilkinson, Richard; Pickett, Kate (2010-04-23). The Spirit Level: Why Greater Equality Makes Societies Stronger (Kindle Locations 227-230). Bloomsbury Publishing Plc. Kindle Edition.

The Author

Laurence De Rusha

I was blown away when I discovered I was born just miles from and eight months after the original Roswell UFO crash. If that wasn't intriguing enough, in 1948 we moved to Aztec, New Mexico, shortly before the other reported UFO crash.

My life has been interesting. I had polio, a near-death experience, and cancer three times. I worked in fusion energy research at Gulf General Atomic Corp., in research and development of some of Wilhelm Reich's unique projects, and have 40 years of research in consciousness and the science of spirituality. I am a Religious Science minister, and researcher for LACCRS Science of Spirituality organization and hold a doctorate of science.

Made in the USA
San Bernardino, CA
01 February 2014